SO-AIK-595

Look What Came From

India

by
Miles Harvey

Franklin Watts
A Division of Scholastic Inc.
New York Toronto London Auckland Sydney
Mexico City New Delhi Hong Kong
Danbury, Connecticut

Series Concept: Shari Joffe
Design: Steve Marton

Library of Congress Cataloging-in-Publication Data

Harvey, Miles.
  Look What Came From India / by Miles Harvey.
    p. cm. — (Look what came from)
  Includes bibliographical references and index.
  Summary: Describes many familiar things that originally
came from India, including inventions, food, religions,
animals, musical instruments, medicine, games, words,
and fashion.
    ISBN 0-531-11587-9   0-531-15965-5 (pbk.)
    1. India—Juvenile literature.   2. India-Social life and
customs. [1. India—Civilization.   2. Civilization—India
influences.] I. Title.   II. Series.
    DS407.H275   1999
    954—dc21
                                                98-35851
                                                  CIP
                                                  AC

Photographs ©: Animals Animals: 19 left (Zig Leszczynski); Art Resource, NY: cover bottom left, 21 right (Victoria & Albert Museum,/London) : 6, 8 right (Borromeo); Chip and Rosa Maria de la Cueva Peterson: 4 left, 10 left, 12 left; Corbis-Bettmann: 7 bottom (Baldwin H. Ward), 3, 23 right; Dinodia Picture Agency: 14 right (Jagdish Agarwal) : cover bottom right, 15, 27 (Viren Desai), 13 top, 22 left (Milind Ketkar), 20 (H. Mahidhar), border on pages.4 and 6-32 (M. M. Navalkar), 4 center (Rajesh H. Sharma), cover top right, 7 top (Ravi Shekkar), 1, 4 right, 10 top right, 11 right, 13 bottom, 21 left, 23 center, 24 left; ENP Images: 18 left (E. A. Kuttapan BBC-NHU), 24 right (Gerry Ellis); E. T. Archive: 14 left (Victoria & Albert Museum); NHPA: 18 right (Joe Blossom); Nik Wheeler: 12 right; Photo Researchers: 17 bottom (E. Hanumantha Rao), 19 right (Dr. M. P. Kahl), 10 bottom right, 11 left, 26 (Joyce Photographics); Superstock, Inc.: 9 top right, 23 left; Tony Stone Images: cover background (Glen Allison), 8 left (Andrea Booner), 25 bottom left, 32 left, (Anthony Cassidy), 25 top left (Peter Correz), 9 top left (Will Curtis), 9 bottom (Nicholas DeVore), 21 center (Greg Pease), 17 top (Manoj Shah), 16 (Joel Simon), 25 right (Chris Simpson), 22 right (Jerome Tisne).

© 1999 Franklin Watts, A Division of Scholastic Inc.
All rights reserved. Published simultaneously in Canada.
Printed in the United States of America.
    6 7 8 9 10 R 08 07 06 05 04 03

Contents

Greetings from India!

India is a country located on the continent of Asia. It has more people than any other country except China. In fact, one out of every six people in the world lives in this amazing place! But that's not the only interesting thing about India. It is also one of the oldest countries on Earth, with a civilization that goes back 5,000 years. Many things in your everyday life— from pajamas to pepper to Parcheesi— come from this fascinating land. So, come on! Let's look at all the cool things that come from India!

Indian paper money and coin

The flag of India

4

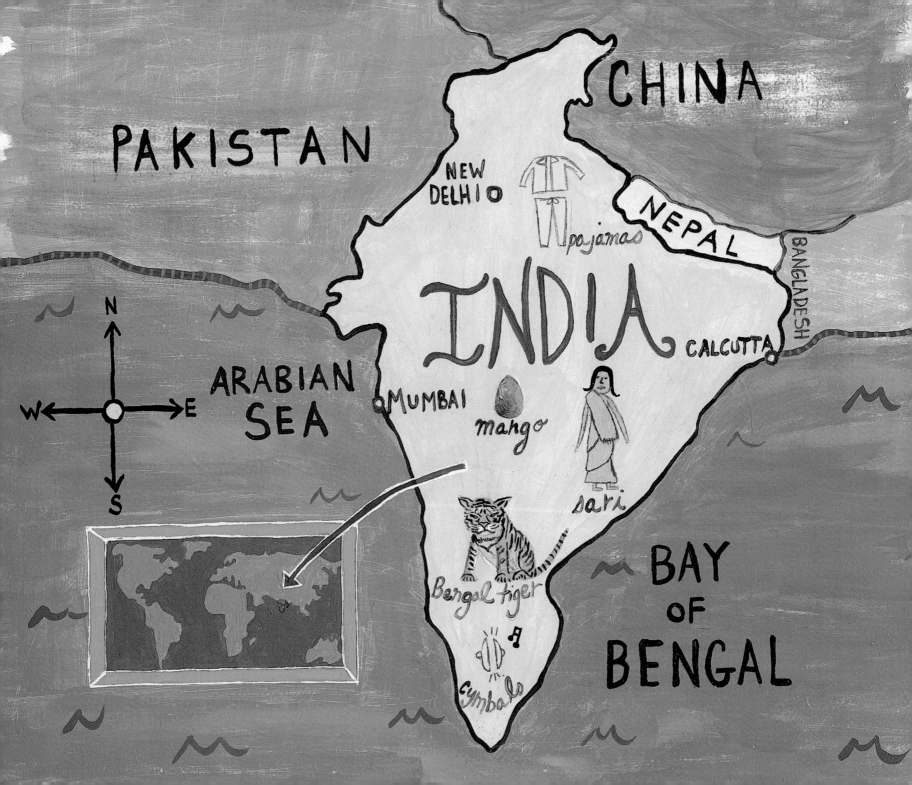

Inventions

The first **bathrooms** were invented in ancient India about 4,500 years ago. Houses in an ancient city called Mohenjo-Daro had little rooms with drains in the floor. People would wash themselves with buckets of water, and the water would go down the drain. Residents of this city also created the first **toilets** that you could sit down on. They were made of bricks and had wooden seats.

The ruins of Mohenjo-Daro

No one knows who invented the first **coins.** But some of the oldest coins in the world have been found in India. These coins are more than 2,500 years old.

Ancient Indian coins

Henri Pecquet in the first airmail plane

The first real **airmail** flight took place in India. A pilot named Henri Pecquet delivered letters from one part of India to another in 1911. That was just eight years after the airplane was invented!

Religion

A Hindu temple

Several of the great religions of the world were started in India. One of these is **Hinduism,** which began about 3,500 years ago. The basic beliefs of this religion are that there are many gods, and that after people die, they are born over and over again into different lives. Today, Hinduism is the most popular religion in India. But there are also millions of Hindus

Hindu women

in other countries. In fact, Hinduism is one of the world's biggest religions, with more than 700 million people.

Young Buddhist monk making a drawing of Buddha

Jainism began in India about 2,500 years ago. Jainists believe that people should never harm any living things. Today, there are about 4 million Jains, and most of them live in India. Another Indian religion is **Sikhism,** which combines parts of the Muslim and Hindu faiths, and believes in one god. It has about 20 million members.

Sikh man

Jain worshippers inside a temple

Buddhism also got started in India. It was founded about 2,500 years ago by a religious leader known as the Buddha. Buddhists believe in living a simple life. This religion is no longer really popular in India, but it remains a very important religion in countries such as Japan.

Man cutting sugarcane in India

Pepper comes from the berry of the pepper plant.

Food

People in India were the first to eat **sugar.** They have been making sugar from the sugarcane plant for as long as 5,000 years. **Pepper** also comes from India.

Vegetarian Indian meal

Mangoes

Another wonderful food that grew first in India is the **mango.** Have you ever tasted this sweet, juicy fruit? It's delicious!

People in India also came up with the idea of **vegetarianism.** People who are vegetarians don't eat any meat. Many people from the Hindu, Buddhist, and Jain religions believe that it is wrong to eat food made from animals.

Today, people in India eat many yummy kinds of foods. You can taste them yourself at an Indian restaurant. One of these delicious meals is a soup called **dhal.** It is made out of lentil beans. Another great dish is called **tandoori chicken.** It is cooked in a very hot clay oven called a tandoor.

more food

Dhal served with rice and a chapati

Tandoori chicken

Indian food served with chapatis

Many kinds of wonderful bread also come from India. One of them is called **chapati.** It is shaped like a pancake and made with a special type of flour.

Indians also love to eat a snack called **bhel puri.** It's made with puffed rice, crispy noodles, and potatoes, and is served with sweet, sour, and spicy sauces.

Bhel puri stand in Mumbai

13

Sixteenth-century Indian painting
showing a man playing cymbals

Musical

Nobody knows who invented **cymbals.**
But experts think they may have originated
in India thousands of years ago.

Another famous instrument that comes
from India is the **sitar.** Have you ever heard
this beautiful instrument? You may have,
even without knowing it.
That's because famous rock
groups such as the Beatles
and the Rolling
Stones use
sitars on
some of their
songs.

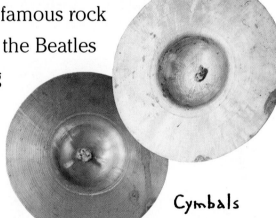

Cymbals

Instruments

Other Indian instruments might be less familiar to you. The **tabla,** for example, is made up of two drums—one that makes high-pitched sounds, and one that makes low-pitched sounds.

Sitar

Tabla

15

Animals

India is home to many famous animals. One of them is a snake called the **Indian cobra.** Its bite is so poisonous that it can kill a human! But some people in India are not afraid of cobras. These people are called snake charmers. They keep the cobras as pets. Snake charmers make money by playing music while a cobra dances around.

Snake charmer with Indian cobra

Indian elephants

Another huge animal is the great **Indian rhinoceros.** Unfortunately, there aren't many of these incredible beasts left. That's because people keep hunting them.

Indian rhinoceros

The **Indian elephant** is found in India and nearby countries. It isn't as big as elephants found in Africa, but that doesn't mean it's small! In fact, Indian elephants can weigh nearly 12,000 pounds (5,400 kg)!

more animals

Bengal tiger

Pygmy hog

Human beings have also killed off far too many tigers. Today, there are only about 5,000 tigers in the world—and more than half of them live in India. The type of tiger usually found in India is the **Bengal tiger.**

The Indian government is working hard to make sure these beautiful animals survive.

Some animals that live in India are less well-known. The **pygmy hog,** for example, is the smallest kind of pig in the world. It can be found only in India. Another unusual Indian animal is the **sloth bear.** It weighs as much as 320 pounds (144 kg) — but it loves to eat tiny insects called termites.

Sloth bear

Sarus cranes

To people in India, the **sarus crane** is the symbol of a happy marriage. That's because when a male and female sarus crane choose each other as mates, they stay together for life!

19

Medicine

People in India invented the first **hospitals** about 2,500 years ago. They also came up with some other great ideas about medicine. For example, **plastic surgery** was invented in India more than 2,000 years ago. Plastic surgery helps people change the way they look.

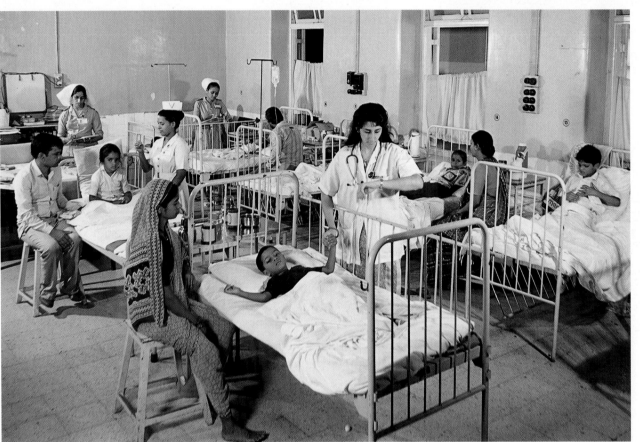

Modern-day hospital in India

Games

Chess

No one knows exactly where the game of **chess** was invented. Some experts think it came from India about 1,400 years ago. But others think it came from Russia even before that.

One game that came from India for sure is **Parcheesi.** It was invented more than 400 years ago. The man who made Parcheesi popular was an Indian emperor named Akbar the Great.

Parcheesi

Akbar the Great (on throne)

21

Pajamas

Fashion

Student wearing traditional Indian pants

Do you wear **pajamas?** The idea for this type of clothing came from India. In fact, the word "pajama" comes from a Hindi word for "pants." These pants look a lot like our pajama bottoms. People in India, however, wear them during the day instead of at night!

Women wearing saris

Do you know what a **cummerbund** is? It's a kind of cloth worn around the waist. Men often wear cummerbunds with tuxedos. The idea for the cummerbund comes from India. So does the word itself.

Another kind of clothing that comes from India is the **Nehru jacket.** It is named after Jawaharlal Nehru, a great Indian political leader. He was famous for wearing this type of jacket.

Rajiv Gandhi, India's prime minister from 1984 to 1989, wearing a Nehru jacket

Another famous kind of Indian clothing is the **sari.** Saris are long pieces of cloth, often made out of beautiful fabrics. Women wrap them around their waists and drape them over their shoulders to form a kind of dress.

23

Words

Shampooing

Many people in India speak English. But this huge land also has 15 other official languages! The main one is called Hindi. We get many of our words from this language. For example, the word **"shampoo"** is based on a Hindi word. **"Jungle"** is also based on a Hindi word.

Jungle

Dungarees

Catamaran

Have you ever worn **"dungarees"**? Maybe so. Dungarees are the same thing as blue jeans. This word also comes from Hindi. Another word that comes from this language is **"guru."** A guru is a religious leader or teacher.

Another language spoken in India is

Guru

Tamil. We get the word **"catamaran"** from this language. A catamaran is a kind of sailboat that has twin hulls.

25

A Recipe from India

Mango Lassi

People in India love a cold drink called mango lassi. This yummy drink is made from yogurt and mangoes and tastes a little bit like a milkshake. You can make it yourself!

To start, you'll need the following ingredients:

1 cup of plain yogurt

1/3 cup of canned mango pulp (You should be able to find mango pulp in the canned-fruits section of the supermarket)

1/2 cup of ice

2 teaspoons of sugar

You'll also need the following equipment:

an electric blender

a measuring cup

a measuring spoon

2 glasses

1. Wash your hands.

2. Measure out the yogurt, mango pulp, ice, and sugar, then pour them into the blender.

3. Adjust the blender or food processor to the "blend" setting.

4. Blend the mixture for one minute.

5. Carefully pour the mixture into the serving glasses.

6. Give it a taste. You're drinking mango lassi!

How do you say....?

Many people in India speak English. But that is far from the only language spoken in this huge country. In fact, there are at least 16 different languages spoken in India! The most popular one is called Hindi. Look how different Hindi words look from English words!

English	Hindi	How to pronounce it
hello (or goodbye)	नमस्ते	nuh-muhs-tay
yes	जी हां	jee-hah
no	जी नहीं	jee-nuh-hee
please	कृपया होगी	krih-pah hoh-gee
thank you	धन्यवाद	duhn-yuh-vahd
chess	शतरंज	shuht-ruhnj
pepper	मिर्च	mirch
sugar	चीनी	chee-nee
vegetarian	शाकाहारी	shah-kah-hah-ree

To find out more

Here are some other resources to help you learn more about India:

Books

Haskins, James. **Count Your Way Through India.** Carolhoda Books, 1990.

Hermes, Jules M. **The Children of India.** Lerner Publications, 1994.

Kalman, Bobbie. **India: The Culture.** Crabtree Publishing, 1989.

Kalman, Bobbie. **India: The Land.** Crabtree Publishing, 1989.

Kalman, Bobbie. **India: The People.** Crabtree Publishing, 1989.

Organizations and Online Sites

Citynet—India
http://www.city.net/countries/india/
Find out today's weather in India—and discover a great list of web links about the country.

I Love India
http://www.iloveindia.com/
Listen to songs at the virtual jukebox and view pictures of modern India.

Map of India
http://www.lib.utexas.edu/Libs/PCL/Map_collection/middle_east_and_asia/India_rel96.jpg
Check out this online map of India, provided by the University of Texas at Austin.

U.S. Embassy of the Government of India
2107 Massachusetts Avenue, NW
Washington, DC 20008
http://www.indianembassy.org/index.html

Government of India Tourist Office
1270 Avenue of Americas, Suite 1808
New York, NY 10020
http://www.tourindia.com/

Glossary

airmail a fast way of delivering mail by using airplanes

catamaran a sailboat that has two hulls

chapati a round, flat Indian bread that is cooked on a griddle

civilization the way of life of a people

continent one of the major land areas of Earth

cummerbund a thick strip of cloth worn around the waist

cymbal a musical instrument made of a round metal plate that makes a ringing sound when struck

hull the body of a boat

mango a tasty tropical fruit with orange pulp

monk a man who has taken religious vows and lives separately with other monks

Parcheesi a board game invented in India more than 400 years ago

plastic surgery a type of medical operation that helps people change the way they look

resident a person who lives in a place

sitar An Indian stringed instrument that has a long neck

sugarcane a plant used to make sugar

tabla a musical instrument made of a high-pitched drum and a low-pitched drum

vegetarian a person who doesn't eat any meat